Y0-CPB-937

Pray Daily: Igniting our Passion for God
A 90-Day Adventure in Prayer

Editor:
E. Stanley Ott

Pray Daily: Igniting Our Passion for God

© 2010 Vital Churches Institute, Inc.

Published by
Vital Churches Institute
P.O. Box 18378
Pittsburgh, PA 15236
www.vitalchurchesinstitute.com
412.246.4847

ISBN: 978-1-931551-11-3

All scripture passages, unless otherwise noted, are taken from the
New Revised Standard Version (NRSV) © 1989,
Division of Christian Education of the National Council of the Churches of Christ in the USA.
Used by permission. All rights reserved.

"One day Jesus was praying in a certain place. When he finished, one of his disciples said to him, 'Lord, teach us to pray.'"
Luke 11.1 NIV

BEHOLD, I AM ABOUT TO DO A NEW THING!
NOW IT SPRINGS FORTH; DO YOU NOT PERCEIVE IT?
ISAIAH 43:19

God is doing a new thing in our church, and that new thing is us! Our Lord wants to make us new creatures, to transform us into the very likeness of Jesus so that we may be completely awakened to God and awakened to do God's work in the world.

God invites us to pursue God's presence through prayer. God responds to such seeking with an unmistakeable presence in our lives, an experience known as an "awakening." The work of the Holy Spirit in our awareness of sin, our enjoyment of grace and our alertness to the presence of God are heightened and intensified.

i

→ Rather than simply being a set of doctrines, religious practices and denominational loyalties, faith begins to shine through the hearts and lives of Christians, and they become a vibrant community irresistible to outsiders. Like Jesus, they love the world with God's love, which brings new life. Surrounding communities are transformed, social injustices are overturned and the Kingdom of God spreads. This is the missional work of God.

In our yearning to become such a community – a joyful, contagious, Christ-centered community devoted to loving and serving God and our neighbors – we have been given the opportunity to seek after God's presence through ninety days of concerted prayer.

Imagine an entire church community committed to praying wherever they are each day for ninety days to enter into God's presence!

What would happen if everyone connected with two others for a time of reflection and prayer? What would that community learn about God and God's mission in the world? About themselves? Their loved ones? How would that community be changed? What impact would that leave on the surrounding community? In the wider world?

Our culture exalts the individual and self-reliance. Self-centeredness is our natural condition. We believe we can accomplish anything through our own efforts, a notion contrary to what we learn in Scripture. God is the prime mover and all we do that is fruitful happens as we are connected to Jesus, the Vine, and dependent on our Lord's blessing.

God, who has already called us with the whole church into relationship, desires for us to go deeper.

- This depth results in transformed lives when we surrender to God, seek God's truth, and receive God's grace, peace, and joy as disciples. Prayer is central to that process.

- God desires to transform us into the people of God, a reflection of Jesus. Prayer is central to that process.

- God, who sends us into the world just as Jesus was sent, desires that we seek God's will and God's kingdom on earth as it is in heaven. Prayer is central to that process.

The framework for this ninety days of prayer experience is based on Jesus' response to his disciples' appeal, "Lord teach us to pray!"

Prayer is a conversation with God and God's beloved people. Jesus instructs us to pray the pattern of the Lord's Prayer for a purpose – we come before our loving God, not as equals, but as children who praise and honor God first.

During the first six weeks, one week will be spent focusing on each aspect of the pattern Jesus teaches: Our Father…Your Kingdom come…Your will be done… Give us this day…Forgive us as…Lead us not into temptation.

During the second six weeks, the pattern is turned into a daily rhythm for prayer:

Sunday	Worship and Rest
Monday	Praise and Adoration
Tuesday	God's Work in the World
Wednesday	God's Work in Us
Thursday	Petitions
Friday	Forgiveness and Confession
Saturday	Protection

We will learn how to read, reflect and respond to God's word as we pray about the issues on our hearts. St. Augustine saw meditation as "the soul's ascent into God." When we meditate on scripture, we pray the truth until it holds us personally, shapes our thinking, changes our emotions and drives our actions. We move from knowing "about" God to knowing God directly from the heart. We adore, marvel, rest in God. We are humbled, troubled, changed and given peace as we pray.

This ninety-day adventure will offer you the opportunity to experience new dimensions in your personal prayer life. You will also experience the joy of praying with two other people for an extended period of time and discover the new depth in personal friendship that takes root.

This booklet is designed for personal, ministry team and congregational use.

For Personal Use: Use the daily guide to pray every day for the ninety days. The guide will offer you a biblical text to read and reflect on, encourage you to respond to that text in your life, and invite you to identify prayer requests and to pray.

For Ministry Team Use: Ask the members of the group, committee, board or ministry team to get into trios – groups of three who will pray for each other daily using this booklet as a guide. For the greatest spiritual impact ask these trios to meet weekly for one hour of Word-Share-Prayer (described in detail on page ix).

Minimally, ask the members of the trios to spend a few minutes after every gathering to touch base and offer updates on previous prayer requests and suggest new prayer requests to their trio members.

For Congregational Use: Dedicating ninety days to prayer is a wonderful way to involve a significant proportion of your congregation in an experience in prayer and in prayer partnerships. This involves three simple steps with appropriate leadership and publicity for each step.

Step One: Conduct an opening celebration for the ninety-day experience (typically Sunday evening).

Step Two: At the gathering form prayer trios – groups of three – which meet weekly for Word-Share-Prayer.

Step Three: Conduct a closing gathering for all participants to celebrate this committed experience to prayer and praying together (typically Sunday evening).

Select a date to celebrate the beginning of the ninety days of prayer.

Step One: Affirmation of Prayer (a one-hour gathering to begin the adventure).

For the month before the opening celebration, lift up the coming ninety days experience with prayer during worship and gatherings using additional publicity as well. Invite people publicly and personally to attend the opening one-hour gathering.

Host the affirmation of prayer on a Sunday evening (or at a good time for the congregation). Begin with hymns and worship songs. Explain the vision of the prayer trios and affirm the privilege, power and joy of praying with other Christians. Explain what the prayer trios will do during the coming ninety days (see Step Two). Ask people to stand and get into trios (helping one another to do so as needed).

Encourage participants to seek trio partners who are different. Wonderful trios have people of differing ages, mixed genders, people who are not already best friends or are related to each other. While this is not always possible, the goal is to connect with a wider circle of people. As the old Girl Scout song says, "Make new friends but keep the old. One is silver and the other gold." Trios move people from silver to gold!

When the trios have formed, ask them to sit, share a prayer request, pray for each other and then set the date of their first trio gathering.

Step Two: Prayer Trios (one hour a week).

Each trio meets every week for one hour at a time mutually agreeable to everyone. The format of the gathering is "Word-Share-Prayer."

"Word" – each one of the trio speaks about the Scripture reading from the last week that has been most meaningful and why.

"Share" – each one shares a blessing from the last week which affirms God's work in their lives and shares a prayer request where the blessing of God is sought.

"Prayer" – each one has the opportunity to pray out loud for at least one other member of the trio, although no one is required to pray out loud.

Step Three: Celebration of Prayer for the participants and congregation (one hour close to the end of the ninety days).

> Opening music – select hymns and worship songs appropriate for a celebration of prayer.
>
> Two or three people share how God answered prayer and how the experience affected them.
>
> Words from the pastor or another leader.
>
> Closing music.

For more Word-Share-Prayer studies that are especially useful for small groups, committees, ministry teams and boards, please go to "Resources" at www.vitalchurchesinstitute.com.

We are grateful to the ministry of the Vienna Presbyterian Church of Vienna, Virginia, where the basic studies of this booklet were first used in the adventure of Ninety Days of Prayer!

Thine Is the Kingdom and the Glory Forever.

Pray Daily: Igniting Our Passion for God

Our Father who art in heaven,
Hallowed be thy name.
Thy Kingdom come,
Thy will be done,
On earth as it is in heaven.
Give us this day our daily bread;
And forgive us our debts,
As we forgive our debtors;
And lead us not into temptation,
But deliver us from evil.
For thine is the kingdom and the power and the glory, forever.
Amen.

Pray Daily: Igniting Our Passion for God

Make a joyful noise to the Lord, all the earth.
Worship the Lord with gladness; Come into his presence with singing.
Know that the Lord is God.
It is he that made us and we are his;
We are his people and the sheep of his pasture.
Enter his gates with thanksgiving, And his courts with praise.
Give thanks to him and bless his name.
For the Lord is good; His steadfast love endures forever.
Psalm 100

REFLECT

What does it mean to know that you belong to God?

RESPOND

Gladly praise God for his goodness. Thank him for three things he has done for you this week. Share your thoughts with another.

PRAY

Lift to God that which is on your heart today.

For from him and through him and to him are all things.
To him be the glory forever! Amen.
Romans 11:36

REflECT

Everything I am and everything I have is from God. Do you believe this?

RESPOND

Seek and find your identity and purpose in God alone.

PRAY

Lift to God that which is on your heart today.

Pray Daily: Igniting Our Passion for God

Who is like you, O Lord, among the gods?
Who is like you, majestic in holiness,
Awesome in splendor, doing wonders?
You stretched out your right hand, the earth swallowed them.
In your steadfast love you led the people whom you redeemed;
You guided them by your strength to your holy abode.
Exodus 15:11-13

REFLECT

How has God demonstrated his steadfast love and led you by his strength to his holy abode? What comes to your mind?

RESPOND

Praise God for his holiness, faithfulness and power in your life. Notice how God is working around you. Tell someone.

PRAY

Lift to God that which is on your heart today.

To the King of the ages, immortal, invisible, the only God,
be honor and glory forever and ever. Amen.
I Timothy 1:17

REFLECT

How is God different from earthly kings?

RESPOND

Give God honor and glory for who he is, the King of kings. What kind of action
could you take to do this?

Lift to God that which is on your heart today. PRAY

Pray Daily: Igniting Our Passion for God

David said: "Blessed are you, O Lord, the God of our ancestor Israel, forever and ever. Yours, O Lord, are the greatness, the power, the glory the victory, and the majesty; for all that is in the heavens and on the earth is yours; yours is the kingdom, O Lord, and you are exalted as head above all. Riches and honor come from you and you rule over all. In your hand are power and might; and it is in your hand to make great and to give strength to all. And now, our God, we give thanks to you and praise your glorious name."
I Chronicles 29:10-13

REFLECT

All riches and honor come from God's glory in you! How does this thought make you feel?

RESPOND

Identify the affections of your heart. Ask God to remove those which detract from God's glory in you.

PRAY

Lift to God that which is on your heart today.

...the twenty-four elders fall before the one who is seated on the throne and worship the one who lives for ever and ever; they cast their crowns before the throne singing, "You are worthy, our Lord and God, to receive glory honor and power, for you created all things, and by your will they existed and were created."
Revelation 4:10-11

REFLECT

Jesus Christ with the Father and the Holy Spirit created all things, and by his will they exist. What does this mean to you?

RESPOND

In what ordinary ways can you give God glory, honor and power in your life?

Lift to God that which is on your heart today.   PRAY

Thine Is the Kingdom and the Glory Forever.

Pray Daily: Igniting Our Passion for God

WEEKLY REFLECTIONS

Our Father who art in heaven,
Hallowed be thy name.
Thy Kingdom come,
Thy will be done,
On earth as it is in heaven.
Give us this day our daily bread;
And forgive us our debts,
As we forgive our debtors;
And lead us not into temptation,
But deliver us from evil.
For thine is the kingdom and the power and the glory, forever.
Amen.

Then God said, "Let us make man in our image, in our likeness, and let them rule over the fish of the sea and the birds of the air, over the livestock, over all the earth, and over the creatures that move along the ground."
Genesis 1:26

REFLECT

God created you to be in perfect fellowship with him and his creation.

RESPOND

Think of three ways to nurture that fellowship and/or how you can care for God's creation.

Lift to God that which is on your heart today.   PRAY

I will make of you a great nation, and I will bless you, and make your name great, so that you will be a blessing. I will bless those who bless you, and the one who curses you I will curse; and in you all the families of the earth shall be blessed.
Genesis 12:2

REFLECT

Think about the many ways God has blessed you and name them aloud.

RESPOND

Resolve to bless at least one other person in a tangible way this week.

Lift to God that which is on your heart today. PRAY

The cry of the Israelites has now come to me; I have also seen how the Egyptians oppress them. So come, I will send you to Pharaoh to bring my people, the Israelites, out of Egypt.

Exodus 3:9-10

REFLECT

Think back on the beginning of your faith journey when God chose you and initiated his kingdom in your life. What do you remember?

RESPOND

How do you need God to intervene in the real circumstances of your life to bring his kingdom in an even greater measure? Pray for it!

PRAY

Lift to God that which is on your heart today.

I myself will be the shepherd of my sheep, and I will make them lie down, says the Lord God. I will seek the lost, and I will bring back the strayed, and I will bind up the injured, and I will strengthen the weak, but the fat and the strong I will destroy. I will feed them with justice.
Ezekiel 34:15-16

REFLECT

Think about God's heart for the lost, the injured and the weak and his desire to feed them.

RESPOND

Pray that God shows you where he is moving and how he wants you to participate in helping those in need this week.

PRAY

Lift to God that which is on your heart today.

Pray Daily: Igniting Our Passion for God

"...for I was hungry and you gave me food, I was thirsty and you gave me something to drink, I was a stranger and you welcomed me, I was naked and you gave me clothing, I was sick and you took care of me, I was in prison and you visited me." Then the righteous will answer him, "Lord, when was it that we saw you hungry and gave you food, or thirsty and gave you something to drink? And when was it that we saw you a stranger and welcomed you, or naked and gave you clothing? And when was it we saw you sick or in prison and visited you?" And the King will reply, "Truly I tell you, just as you did it to one of the least of these who are members of my family, you did it to me."
Matthew 25:34-40

REFLECT

Do you feel loved and blessed by God? What does it mean to inherit the kingdom prepared for us from the foundation of the world?

RESPOND

Do something today just because Jesus commands it.

Lift to God that which is on your heart today. PRAY

The Spirit of the Lord is upon me,
because he has anointed me
to bring good news to the poor.
He has sent me to proclaim release for the captives
and recovery of sight to the blind,
to let the oppressed go free,
to proclaim the year of the Lord's favor.
Luke 4:18-19

REFLECT

Remember a time when you were in need and Jesus released you. Did you transition from blindness to having sight to God's truth?

RESPOND

Do you know someone who is in great spiritual need? How is God calling you to bring them good news? Talk to someone about this.

PRAY

Lift to God that which is on your heart today.

Thine Is the Kingdom and the Glory Forever.

Pray Daily: Igniting Our Passion for God

Our Father who art in heaven,
Hallowed be thy name.
Thy Kingdom come,
Thy will be done,
On earth as it is in heaven.
Give us this day our daily bread;
And forgive us our debts,
As we forgive our debtors;
And lead us not into temptation,
But deliver us from evil.
For thine is the kingdom and the power and the glory, forever.
Amen.

Pray Daily: Igniting Our Passion for God

"Father, if you are willing, remove this cup from me; yet not my will but yours be done."
Luke 22:42

REFLECT

Think about Jesus praying in the garden pleading with his Father and then succumbing to obedience. What are your thoughts and feelings?

RESPOND

What temptations are you facing today? Resolve to surrender these to your loving Father. "Not my will but yours be done."

PRAY

Lift to God that which is on your heart today.

Hear, O Israel: The Lord is our God, the Lord God alone. You shall love the Lord your God with all your heart, and with all your soul, and with all your might. Keep these words that I am commanding you today in your heart. Recite them to your children and talk about them when you are at home and when you are away, when you lie down and when you rise. Bind them as a sign on your hand, fix them as an emblem on your forehead, and write them on the doorposts of your house and on your gates.
Deuteronomy 6:6-9

REFLECT

What does it mean for you to love God with all your heart, soul and might?

RESPOND

Identify three specific ways to keep this command continually in your mind and to pass this love on to those close to you.

Lift to God that which is on your heart today.   PRAY

"This is my commandment, that you love one another as I have loved you. No one has greater love than this, to lay down one's life for one's friends. You are my friends if you do what I command you."
John 15:12-13

REFLECT

How does Jesus love you and use others to show his love to you?

RESPOND

As you consider God's work for you in the world, think of specific ways you keep love central to all you do. Share your ideas with a friend.

Lift to God that which is on your heart today. ## PRAY

Teach me to do your will, for you are my God.
Let your good spirit lead me on a level path.
Psalm 143:10

Say this verse aloud at least five times.

Ask God to lead you on the path of his will today.

Lift to God that which is on your heart today.

REFLECT
RESPOND
PRAY

Pray Daily: Igniting Our Passion for God

The angel said to her, "Do not be afraid, Mary, for you have found favor with God. And now you will conceive in your womb and bear a son and you will name him Jesus." Then Mary said, "Here I am, the servant of the Lord; let it be with me according to your word."
Luke 1:30-31

REFLECT

How did Mary feel upon receiving this message from the angel? What did it mean for her to surrender to God's will as she did?

RESPOND

Ask God to show you his will and surrender to it.

Lift to God that which is on your heart today. PRAY

Trust in the Lord with all your heart,
And do not rely on your own insight.
In all your ways acknowledge him
And he will make straight your paths.
Proverbs 3:5-6

REFLECT

Focus on what it means to trust God alone in everything.

RESPOND

Ask God to show you his ways on your path today.

PRAY

Lift to God that which is on your heart today.

Thine Is the Kingdom and the Glory Forever.

Pray Daily: Igniting Our Passion for God

Our Father who art in heaven,
Hallowed be thy name.
Thy Kingdom come,
Thy will be done,
On earth as it is in heaven.
Give us this day our daily bread;
And forgive us our debts,
As we forgive our debtors;
And lead us not into temptation,
But deliver us from evil.
For thine is the kingdom and the power and the glory, forever.
Amen.

Come to me, all you that are weary and are carrying heavy burdens, and I will give you rest. Take my yoke upon you, and learn from me, for I am gentle and humble in heart, and you will find rest for your souls. For my yoke is easy, and my burden is light.
Matthew 11:28-30

REFLECT

Jesus is inviting you to give him your worries and rest in him.
How does this make you feel?

RESPOND

Turn over a struggle to Jesus. Allow him to carry it and show you how to walk with or through it. Share your experience with a brother or sister in Christ.

Lift to God that which is on your heart today. PRAY

He said to his disciples, "Therefore I tell you, do not worry about your life, what you will eat, or about your body, what you will wear. For life is more than food, and the body more than clothing."
Luke 12:22-23

REFLECT

Think about how God has provided for you in the past.

RESPOND

Resolve to set your mind on God's goodness and promise of provision rather than setting your mind on the things that worry you.

Lift to God that which is on your heart today. PRAY

Pray Daily: Igniting Our Passion for God

Rejoice in the Lord always; again I say rejoice. Let your gentleness be known to everyone. The Lord is near. Do not worry about anything but in everything by prayer and supplication with thanksgiving let your requests be made known to God. And the peace of God which surpasses all understanding, will guard your hearts and minds in Christ Jesus.
Philippians 4:4-7

REFLECT

What about Jesus makes you joyful?

RESPOND

Rejoice in all God has done for you and pray about your present needs.

Lift to God that which is on your heart today. PRAY

Teach me your way, O Lord,
That I may walk in your truth;
Give me an undivided heart to revere your name.
Psalm 86:11

REflECT

Do you know what draws your heart away from God?

RESPOND

Ask God to teach you his way and give you an undivided heart to trust his plans for your life.

Lift to God that which is on your heart today.   PRAY

Pray Daily: Igniting Our Passion for God

...a thorn was given to me in the flesh, a messenger of Satan to torment me, to keep me from being too elated. Three times I appealed to the Lord about this, that it would leave me, but he said to me, "My grace is sufficient for you, for my power is made perfect in weakness." So I will boast all the more gladly of my weakness, so that the power of Christ may dwell in me.

2 Corinthians 12:7-9

REFLECT

In what circumstances are you aware of your need for God's grace to accomplish for you what you cannot accomplish on your own?

RESPOND

Trust God's power in your life today!

PRAY

Lift to God that which is on your heart today.

"As you Father are in me and I am in you, may they also be in us, so that the world may believe that you have sent me. The glory that you have given me I have given them, so that they may be one, as we are one, I in them and you in me, that they may become completely one, so that the world may know that you have sent me and have loved them even as you have loved me."
John 17:20-23

REFLECT

Think about the unity we share with God and with other believers.

RESPOND

Pray for this unity to be lived out in our relationships in families and in the church community so that the world may see the love of Jesus in us.

Lift to God that which is on your heart today. PRAY

Thine Is the Kingdom and the Glory Forever.

Pray Daily: Igniting Our Passion for God

Our Father who art in heaven,
Hallowed be thy name.
Thy Kingdom come,
Thy will be done,
On earth as it is in heaven.
Give us this day our daily bread;
And forgive us our debts,
As we forgive our debtors;
And lead us not into temptation,
But deliver us from evil.
For thine is the kingdom and the power and the glory, forever.
Amen.

Pray Daily: Igniting Our Passion for God

But the Lord God called to the man, and said to him, "Where are you?" He said, "I heard the sound of you in the garden, and I was afraid, because I was naked; and I hid myself." He said, "Who told you that you were naked? Have you eaten from the tree which I commanded you not to eat?" The man said, "The woman whom you gave to be with me, she gave me the fruit from the tree, and I ate." Then the Lord God said to the woman, "What is this that you have done?" The woman said, "The serpent tricked me, and I ate."

Genesis 3:8-13

REFLECT

Think about how challenging it was for Adam and Eve to have been confronted by God in their disobedience.

RESPOND

Ask the Holy Spirit to reveal your sin. What acts of disobedience do you need to take responsibility for before God? Take them to God.

Lift to God that which is on your heart today. PRAY

And Moses quickly bowed his head toward the earth, and worshipped. He said, "If now I have found favor in your sight, O Lord, I pray, let the Lord go with us. Although this is a stiff-necked people, pardon our iniquity and our sin, and take us for your inheritance."
Exodus 34:8-9

REFLECT

To leave one place is to head toward something else. Know that God goes with us and he takes us as his people.

RESPOND

Ask God to show you what you need to change to gain favor in his sight. Ask the Holy Spirit to change you in this area.

Lift to God that which is on your heart today. PRAY

I will sprinkle clean water upon you, and you shall be clean from all your uncleanness, and from all your idols I will cleanse you. A new heart I will give you, and a new spirit I will put within you; and I will remove from your body the heart of stone and give you a heart of flesh. I will put my spirit within you, and make you follow my statutes and be careful to observe my ordinances. Then you shall live in the land I gave your ancestors; and you shall be my people, and I will be your God.

Ezekiel 36:25-28

REFLECT

How is your heart hard? In what ways are you unclean?

RESPOND

Confess this to God so that you can stand before him clean and with boldness to do his work in the world.

Lift to God that which is on your heart today. ## PRAY

If we say that we have no sin, we deceive ourselves, and the truth is not in us.
If we confess our sins, he who is faithful and just will forgive us and our sins
and cleanse us from all our unrighteousness.
I John 1:8-9

REFLECT

What actions have you minimized or failed to confess as sin?

RESPOND

Confess and believe the Good News in Jesus Christ that you are forgiven.

PRAY

Lift to God that which is on your heart today.

In him we have redemption through his blood, the forgiveness of our trespasses, according to the riches of his grace.
Ephesians 1:7

REFLECT

Ponder this verse throughout the day.

RESPOND

What sins have you confessed but still feel guilty for? Believe God and ask him to show you the cleansing power that comes only by his grace.

Lift to God that which is on your heart today.   PRAY

Then Jesus said, "Father, forgive them; for they know not what they are doing."
Luke 23:34

REfLECT

Consider the great compassion of Jesus looking on those who were crucifying
him.

RESPOND

Whom do you need to forgive? Ask God to enable you to forgive with
compassion as he does.

Lift to God that which is on your heart today. PRAY

Thine Is the Kingdom and the Glory Forever.

Our Father who art in heaven,
Hallowed be thy name.
Thy Kingdom come,
Thy will be done,
On earth as it is in heaven.
Give us this day our daily bread;
And forgive us our debts,
As we forgive our debtors;
And lead us not into temptation,
But deliver us from evil.
For thine is the kingdom and the power and the glory, forever.
Amen.

Pray Daily: Igniting Our Passion for God

So if you think you are standing, watch out that you do not fall. No testing has overtaken you that is not common to everyone. God is faithful, and he will not let you be tested beyond your strength, but with the testing he will also provide the way out so that you may be able to endure it.
I Corinthians 10:12-13

REFLECT

Recall one or two specific times when God sustained you and provided a way out of difficulties you thought were too great to bear.

RESPOND

Resolve to be alert today for a fresh example in your life of God's faithfulness and protection when you are tempted.

Lift to God that which is on your heart today. PRAY

Blessed is anyone who endures temptation. Such a one has stood the test and will receive the crown of life that the Lord has promised to those who love him. No one, when tempted, should say, "I am being tempted by God" for God cannot be tempted by evil and he himself tempts no one.

James 1:12-13

REFLECT

Memorize this! How has God shown you his love in the face of evil?

RESPOND

The next time temptation comes your way, consciously remind yourself that it does not come from God.

PRAY

Lift to God that which is on your heart today.

Pray Daily: Igniting Our Passion for God

...then the Lord knows how to rescue the godly from trial, and to keep the unrighteous under punishment until the day of judgment....
2 Peter 2:9

REFLECT

Write down this verse and read it over several times today.

RESPOND

Praise God that he is able to rescue from trials those who love him.

Lift to God that which is on your heart today. PRAY

Our soul waits for the Lord;
He is our help and shield.
Psalm 33:20

REFLECT

Remember a time when you waited on the Lord's help and protection.

RESPOND

Attune yourself today to watch for God's delivery of you by his promise.

Lift to God that which is on your heart today. PRAY

Pray Daily: Igniting Our Passion for God

O my strength I will watch for you;
For you, O God, are my fortress.
Psalm 59:9

REflECT

Think and pray about the image of God as a fortress.

RESPOND

When you are tested, bring to mind the image that "God is my fortress."

Lift to God that which is on your heart today.   PRAY

The name of the Lord is a strong tower,
The righteous run into it and are safe.
Proverbs 18:10

REFLECT

Imagine God as a strong tower, a place of safety.

RESPOND

Put God's promise to work for you in prayer by calling on his name today as your strong tower.

Lift to God that which is on your heart today. PRAY

Thine Is the Kingdom and the Glory Forever.

Pray Daily: Igniting Our Passion for God

WEEKLY REFLECTIONS

Our Father who art in heaven,
Hallowed be thy name.
Thy Kingdom come,
Thy will be done,
On earth as it is in heaven.
Give us this day our daily bread;
And forgive us our debts,
As we forgive our debtors;
And lead us not into temptation,
But deliver us from evil.
For thine is the kingdom and the power and the glory, forever.
Amen.

Pray Daily: Igniting Our Passion for God

And one called to another and said:
"Holy, holy, holy is the Lord of hosts;
The whole earth is full of his glory."
Isaiah 6:3

REFLECT

Memorize this verse.

RESPOND

Praise God for his holiness.

PRAY

Lift to God that which is on your heart today.

And Jesus came and said to them, "All authority in heaven and on earth has been given to me. Go therefore and make disciples of all nations, baptizing them in the name of the Father and of the Son and of the Holy Spirit, and teaching them to obey everything that I have commanded you. And remember, I am with you always, to the end of the age."
Matthew 28:18-20

REFLECT

How are you obeying Jesus' command to make disciples?

RESPOND

What is your next step to join in God's work to make disciples?

PRAY

Lift to God that which is on your heart today.

I appeal to you...by the mercies of God, to present your bodies as a living sacrifice, holy and acceptable to God, which is your spiritual worship. Do not be conformed to this world, but be transformed by the renewing of your minds, so that you may discern what is the will of God – what is good and acceptable and perfect.

Romans 12:1-2

REFLECT

Ponder what it means to present your body as a living sacrifice.

RESPOND

Memorize part of this Bible passage. Resist conformity to this world.

Lift to God that which is on your heart today.   PRAY

I pray...he may grant that you may be strengthened in your inner being with power through his Spirit, and that Christ may dwell in your hearts through faith, as you are being rooted and grounded in love. I pray that you may have the power to comprehend, with all the saints, what is the breadth and length and height and depth, and to know the love of Christ that surpasses knowledge, so that you may be filled with all the fullness of God.
Ephesians 3:16-19

REFLECT

Consider the breadth, length, height and depth of Christ's love for you.

RESPOND

Ask God to fill with you a deeper awareness of his love for you.

Lift to God that which is on your heart today. PRAY

...let your ear be attentive and your eyes open to hear the prayer of your servant that I now pray before you day and night for your servants, the people of Israel, confessing the sins of the people of Israel, which we have sinned against you. Both I and my family have sinned. We have offended you deeply, failing to keep the commandments, the statutes, and the ordinances that you commanded your servant Moses.
Nehemiah 1:6-7

REFLECT

Like Nehemiah, confess your own sin and the sins of your people.

RESPOND

Ask God to forgive you.

Lift to God that which is on your heart today.   PRAY

Though I walk in the midst of trouble
You preserve me against the wrath of my enemies;
You stretch out your hand,
And your right hand delivers me.
Psalm 138:7

REFLECT

In a world where hate and evil surround us, as individuals and as a nation, think of God's promise to preserve us.

RESPOND

List three troubles in your life right now; ask God to deliver you – as he promised he will do.

PRAY

Lift to God that which is on your heart today.

Thine Is the Kingdom and the Glory Forever.

WEEKLY REFLECTIONS

Our Father who art in heaven,
Hallowed be thy name.
Thy Kingdom come,
Thy will be done,
On earth as it is in heaven.
Give us this day our daily bread;
And forgive us our debts,
As we forgive our debtors;
And lead us not into temptation,
But deliver us from evil.
For thine is the kingdom and the power and the glory, forever.
Amen.

Now to him who by the power at work within us is able to accomplish abundantly far more than all we can ask or imagine, to him be the glory in the church and in Christ Jesus to all generations, for ever and ever. Amen.
Ephesians 3:20-21

REFLECT

My God is able to accomplish abundantly more than I can ask for or imagine.

RESPOND

Praise God and give him glory for his great love and power.

PRAY

Lift to God that which is on your heart today.

Very truly, I tell you the one who believes in me will also do the works that I do and, in fact, will do greater works than these, because I am going to the Father. I will do whatever you ask in my name, so that the Father may be glorified in the Son. If in my name you ask me for anything, I will do it.
John 14:12-14

REFLECT

Think about the fact that as believers indwelt by the Holy Spirit, we can do great works for God.

RESPOND

Ask God to reveal to you where he is working in the world so that you can join him.

PRAY

Lift to God that which is on your heart today.

I, therefore, the prisoner in the Lord, beg you to lead a life worthy of the calling to which you have been called, with all humility and gentleness, with patience, bearing with one another in love, making every effort to maintain the unity of the Spirit in the bond of peace.
Ephesians 4:1-3

REFLECT

What does it mean for you to lead a life worthy of God's call, with all humility and gentleness?

RESPOND

Identify a difficult relationship and ask God to help you bear with this person in love.

Lift to God that which is on your heart today.   PRAY

"And now, Lord, look at their threats, and grant to your servants to speak your word with all boldness, while you stretch out your hand to heal, and signs and wonders are performed through the name of your holy servant Jesus."
Acts 4:29-30

REFLECT

Think about how these early believers faced real threats, prayed for boldness and trusted God's power to be manifested.

RESPOND

Pray that God will enable you, his servant, to speak his word with all boldness and to trust his power, no matter what your circumstances.

Lift to God that which is on your heart today. PRAY

Put away from you all bitterness and wrath and anger and wrangling and slander, together with all malice, and be kind to one another, tender-hearted, forgiving one another, as God in Christ has forgiven you.
Ephesians 4:31-32

REFLECT

What or whom do you need to forgive?

RESPOND

Extend forgiveness for offenses against you.

PRAY

Lift to God that which is on your heart today.

So then..., we are debtors, not to the flesh, to live according to the flesh – for if you live according to the flesh, you will die; but if by the Spirit you put to death the deeds of the body, you will live. For all who are led by the Spirit of God are children of God. For you did not receive a spirit of slavery to fall back into fear, but you have received a spirit of adoption. When we cry, "Abba! Father!" it is that very Spirit bearing witness with our spirit that we are children of God.
Romans 8:12-16

REFLECT

It is joyful to have God as a loving parent.

RESPOND

Ask God to enable you to be led by the Spirit, therefore resisting any temptations to live according to the flesh.

Lift to God that which is on your heart today. PRAY

Pray Daily: Igniting Our Passion for God

Our Father who art in heaven,
Hallowed be thy name.
Thy Kingdom come,
Thy will be done,
On earth as it is in heaven.
Give us this day our daily bread;
And forgive us our debts,
As we forgive our debtors;
And lead us not into temptation,
But deliver us from evil.
For thine is the kingdom and the power and the glory, forever.
Amen.

Pray Daily: Igniting Our Passion for God

The steadfast love of the Lord never ceases,
His mercies never come to an end;
They are new every morning;
Great is your faithfulness.
Lamentations 3:22-23

REfLECT

Think about God's steadfast love, unending mercy, and great faithfulness.

RESPOND

Praise God by singing "Great Is Thy Faithfulness."

PRAY

Lift to God that which is on your heart today.

So if anyone is in Christ, they are a new creation: everything old has passed away; see, everything has become new! ...God, who reconciled us to himself through Christ, and has given us the ministry of reconciliation; ...God was reconciling the world to himself, not counting their trespasses against them, and entrusting the message of reconciliation to us. So we are ambassadors for Christ, since God is making appeal through us; we entreat you on behalf of Christ, be reconciled to God.

2 Corinthians 5:17-20

REFLECT

What does it mean to be a new creation, reconciled to God?

RESPOND

Where is God calling you to be an ambassador, bringing others to him?

PRAY

Lift to God that which is on your heart today.

As God's chosen ones, holy and beloved, clothe yourselves with compassion, kindness, humility, meekness, and patience. Bear with one another and, if anyone has a complaint against another, forgive each other; just as the Lord has forgiven you, so you also must forgive. Above all, clothe yourselves with love, which binds everything together in perfect harmony. And let the peace of Christ rule in your hearts, to which indeed you were called in the one body. And be thankful.
Colossians 3:12-15

REFLECT

In what ways is your life incongruent with the passage you just read?

RESPOND

Write this passage on a 3x5 card and place it where you can read it daily until you have memorized it.

Lift to God that which is on your heart today. PRAY

First of all, then I urge that supplications, prayers, intercessions, and thanksgivings should be made for everyone, for kings and all who are in high positions, so that we may lead a quiet and peaceable life in all godliness and dignity. This is right and is acceptable in the sight of God our Savior, who desires everyone to be saved and to come to the knowledge of the truth.
1 Timothy 2:1-4

REFLECT

Think about your call to be an intercessor for leaders.

RESPOND

Pray for our political and Christian leaders to lead quiet and peaceable lives in all godliness and dignity.

Lift to God that which is on your heart today.

PRAY

Pray Daily: Igniting Our Passion for God

Put to death, therefore, whatever in you is earthly: fornication, impurity, passion, evil desire, and greed (which is idolatry). On account of these the wrath of God is coming on those who are disobedient. These are the ways you also once followed, when you were living that life. But now you must get rid of all such things – anger, wrath, malice, slander, and abusive language from your mouth. Do not lie to one another, seeing that you have stripped off the old self with its practices and have clothed yourselves with the new self, which is being renewed in knowledge according to the image of its creator.
Colossians 3:5-10

REFLECT

How is the grace I have in Jesus Christ the key to helping me overcome my sin?

RESPOND

Pray for the Holy Spirit to guide you and change you.

PRAY

Lift to God that which is on your heart today.

Finally, beloved, whatever is true, whatever is honorable, whatever is just, whatever is pure, whatever is pleasing, whatever is commendable, if there is any excellence and if there is anything worthy of praise, think about these things. Keep on doing the things that you have learned and received and heard and seen in me, and the God of peace will be with you.
Philippians 4:8-9

REflECT

Are you putting into practice Jesus' teachings?

RESPOND

Ask the Holy Spirit to guide you to activities in your life that will worship and glorify God.

PRAY

Lift to God that which is on your heart today.

Thine Is the Kingdom and the Glory Forever.

WEEKLY REFLECTIONS

Our Father who art in heaven,
Hallowed be thy name.
Thy Kingdom come,
Thy will be done,
On earth as it is in heaven.
Give us this day our daily bread;
And forgive us our debts,
As we forgive our debtors;
And lead us not into temptation,
But deliver us from evil.
For thine is the kingdom and the power and the glory, forever.
Amen.

Therefore God also highly exalted him
And gave him the name
That is above every name,
So that at the name of Jesus
Every knee should bend,
In heaven and on earth and under the earth.
Philippians 2:9-10

REFLECT

If God does this for Jesus, what difference does this make in your life today?

RESPOND

Bow down and humble yourself before God.

Lift to God that which is on your heart today.   PRAY

Then Jesus went about all the cities and villages, teaching in their synagogues, and proclaiming the good news of the kingdom, and curing every disease and every sickness. When he saw the crowds, he had compassion for them, because they were harassed and helpless, like sheep without a shepherd. Then he said to his disciples, "The harvest is plentiful, but the laborers are few."
Matthew 9:35-37

REflECT

What does the Kingdom of God look like?

RESPOND

Look around today for the people God has compassion for and love them like Jesus loves.

PRAY

Lift to God that which is on your heart today.

Pray Daily: Igniting Our Passion for God

Let the word of Christ dwell in you richly; teach and admonish one another in all wisdom; and with gratitude in your hearts sing psalms, hymns, and spiritual songs to God. And whatever you do, in word or deed, do everything in the name of the Lord Jesus, giving thanks to God the Father through him.
Colossians 3:16-17

REFLECT

Let the word of Christ dwell in you richly and translate into new choices and actions.

RESPOND

Ask God to empower you by his Spirit today to "do everything in the name of the Lord Jesus, giving thanks to God the Father through him."

PRAY

Lift to God that which is on your heart today.

She was deeply distressed and prayed to the Lord, and wept bitterly.
1 Samuel 1:10

REFLECT

Picture a loving father's response to his child crying in distress.

RESPOND

Look for people in distress and enter into their distress with love and compassion.

Lift to God that which is on your heart today.

Pray Daily: Igniting Our Passion for God

"...God, keeping covenant and steadfast love with those who love you and keep your commandments, we have sinned and done wrong, acted wickedly and rebelled, turning aside from your commandments and ordinances. We have not listened to your servants the prophets, who spoke in your name to our kings, our princes, and our ancestors, and to all the people of the land."
Daniel 9:4-6

REFLECT

How have you turned aside from God's commandments and ordinances?
How have you not listened to God's servants?

RESPOND

Ask God for a clean conscience so that you can stand before him in confidence to do his work in the world.

PRAY

Lift to God that which is on your heart today.

But those who want to get rich fall into temptation and are trapped by many senseless and harmful desires that plunge people into ruin and destruction. For the love of money is a root of all kinds of evil, and in their eagerness to be rich some have wandered away from the faith and pierced themselves with many pains.

1 Timothy 6:9-10

REFLECT

Focus on the warning God gives us in this passage.

RESPOND

In light of this truth, ask God to show you what wrong behavior, harmful affections, or false attitudes flow in you.

Lift to God that which is on your heart today.   ## PRAY

Pray Daily: Igniting Our Passion for God

Our Father who art in heaven,
Hallowed be thy name.
Thy Kingdom come,
Thy will be done,
On earth as it is in heaven.
Give us this day our daily bread;
And forgive us our debts,
As we forgive our debtors;
And lead us not into temptation,
But deliver us from evil.
For thine is the kingdom and the power and the glory, forever.
Amen.

"Stand up and bless the Lord your God from everlasting to everlasting. Blessed be your glorious name, which is exalted above all blessing and praise." And Ezra said: "You are the Lord, you alone; you have made heaven, the heaven of heavens, with all their host, the earth and all that is on it, the seas and all that is in them. To all of them you give life, and the host of heaven worships you."
Nehemiah 9:5b-6

REFLECT

Think about God giving life to everything.

RESPOND

Using Ezra's prayer, join all of creation in giving praise to God.

PRAY

Lift to God that which is on your heart today.

But you are a chosen race, a royal priesthood, a holy nation, God's own people, in order that you may proclaim the mighty acts of him who called you out of darkness into his marvelous light.
Once you were not a people,
But now you are God's people;
Once you had not received mercy,
But now you have received mercy.
1 Peter 2:9-10

REFLECT

I am part of those chosen to be God's people called out of darkness into his light.

RESPOND

Choose a specific action you can take (today or this week) as God's instrument for his work in the world.

Lift to God that which is on your heart today. PRAY

For this is the will of God, your sanctification; that you abstain from fornication; that each one of you knows how to control your own body in holiness and honor, not with lustful passion, like the Gentiles who do not know God; that no one wrongs or exploits a brother or sister in this matter, because the Lord is an avenger in all these things, just as we have already told you beforehand and solemnly warned you.

1 Thessalonians 4:3

REFLECT

To be sanctified (to become holy), I must control my own body.

RESPOND

Consider fasting from an activity or food item this week.

PRAY

Lift to God that which is on your heart today.

Are any among you suffering? They should pray. Are any cheerful? They should
sing songs of praise. Are any among you sick? They should call for the elders of
the church and have them pray over them, anointing them with oil in the name
of the Lord. The prayer of faith will save the sick, and the Lord will raise them
up; and anyone who has committed sins will be forgiven. Therefore confess
your sins to one another, and pray for one another, so that you may be healed.
They prayer of the righteous is powerful and effective.
James 5:13-16

REFLECT

Identify the greatest need you or someone you know has today.

RESPOND

Join with someone in lifting up that need before the Lord in prayer.

Lift to God that which is on your heart today.   PRAY

Pray Daily: Igniting Our Passion for God

Indeed, under the law almost everything is purified with blood, and without the shedding of blood there is no forgiveness of sins.
Hebrews 9:22

REFLECT

Jesus died for me. His blood was shed to cover my sins.

RESPOND

Offer prayers of gratitude for his cleansing and healing touch.

Lift to God that which is on your heart today.

When he got up from prayer, he came to the disciples and found them sleeping because of grief, and he said to them, "Why are you sleeping? Get up and pray that you may not come into the time of trial."
Luke 22:45-46

REFLECT

What does this encounter with Jesus reveal about human nature?

RESPOND

Get up and pray for God to protect you from temptation.

Lift to God that which is on your heart today. PRAY

Pray Daily: Igniting Our Passion for God

Our Father who art in heaven,
Hallowed be thy name.
Thy Kingdom come,
Thy will be done,
On earth as it is in heaven.
Give us this day our daily bread;
And forgive us our debts,
As we forgive our debtors;
And lead us not into temptation,
But deliver us from evil.
For thine is the kingdom and the power and the glory, forever.
Amen.

"Worthy is the Lamb that was slaughtered
To receive power and wealth and wisdom and might
And honor and glory and blessing!"
Then I heard every creature in heaven and on earth and under the earth and in
the sea, and all that is in them, singing,
"To the one seated on the throne and to the Lamb
Be blessing and honor and glory and might
For ever and ever!"
Revelation 5:12-13

REFLECT

Think about why Jesus the Lamb is worthy.

RESPOND

Slowly read this passage aloud with others to give honor to Christ.

PRAY

Lift to God that which is on your heart today.

Then I saw a new heaven and a new earth; for the first heaven and the first earth had passed away, and the sea was no more. And I saw the holy city, the new Jerusalem, coming down out of heaven from God, prepared as a bride adorned for her husband. And I heard a loud voice from the throne saying, "See, the home of God is among mortals. He will dwell with them; they will be his people, and God himself will be with them; He will wipe every tear from their eyes. Death will be no more; mourning and crying and pain will be no more, for the first things have passed away."
Revelation 21:1-5

REFLECT

If God's Kingdom is like this, what difference does that make on how I live?

RESPOND

Find opportunities to bring God's love to people who are hurting.

Lift to God that which is on your heart today.   PRAY

Pray Daily: Igniting Our Passion for God

Rejoice always, pray without ceasing, give thanks in all circumstances;
For this is the will of God in Christ Jesus for you.
1 Thessalonians 5:18

REFLECT

Memorize this verse and meditate on it this week.

RESPOND

Live out God's will for you this week by obeying the commands in the verse.

PRAY

Lift to God that which is on your heart today.

Then Esther said in reply to Mordecai, "Go, gather all the Jews to be found in Susa, and hold a fast on my behalf, and neither eat nor drink for three days, night or day. I and my maids will also fast as you do. After that I will go to the king, though it is against the law; and if I perish, I perish."
Esther 4:15-16

REFLECT

What does this passage reveal about Esther's faith and devotion to God's work in the world?

RESPOND

Gather people to pray for you as you embark on your next important endeavor.

Lift to God that which is on your heart today.   PRAY

"Woe is me! I am lost, for I am a man of unclean lips, and I live among a people of unclean lips; yet my eyes have seen the King, the Lord of hosts!" Then one of the seraphs flew to me, holding a live coal that had been taken from the altar with a pair of tongs. The seraph touched my mouth with it and said: "Now that this has touched your lips, your guilt has departed and your sin is blotted out."

Isaiah 6:5-7

REflECT

Focus on Isaiah's reaction in the presence of our holy God and God's response.

RESPOND

Humble yourself before God and confess.

Lift to God that which is on your heart today.   PRAY

My friends, if anyone is detected in a transgression, you who have received the Spirit should restore such a one in a spirit of gentleness. Take care that you yourselves are not tempted. Bear one another's burdens, and in this way you will fulfill the law of Christ.
Galatians 6:1-2

REfLECT

What wrongful behavior or harmful emotions or false attitudes result in you when you ignore these truths?

RESPOND

How can you enter into God's work of restoration? Pray for God to give you wisdom and a spirit of gentleness.

Lift to God that which is on your heart today.   PRAY

WEEKLY REFLECTIONS

Our Father who art in heaven,
Hallowed be thy name.
Thy Kingdom come,
Thy will be done,
On earth as it is in heaven.
Give us this day our daily bread;
And forgive us our debts,
As we forgive our debtors;
And lead us not into temptation,
But deliver us from evil.
For thine is the kingdom and the power and the glory, forever.
Amen.

The Lord is my strength and my shield;
In him my heart trusts;
So I am helped, and my heart exults,
And with my song I give thanks to him.
Psalm 28:7

REFLECT

God gives power and protection for his children.

RESPOND

Ask God to enable you to trust him in the circumstances of your life today.

PRAY

Lift to God that which is on your heart today.

You then, my child, be strong in the grace that is Christ Jesus; and what you have heard from me through many witnesses entrust to faithful people who will be able to teach others as well.

2 Timothy 2:1-2

REFLECT

Recall those faithful people God used to teach you and identify those God is calling you to teach.

RESPOND

Thank God for those who have taught you and pray that God will make you a faithful teacher in the lives of others.

Lift to God that which is on your heart today. PRAY

Love is patient; love is kind; love is not envious of boastful or arrogant or rude. It does not insist on its own way; it is not irritable or resentful; it does not rejoice in wrongdoing, but rejoices in the truth. It bears all things, believes all things, hopes all things, endures all things. Love never ends.
1 Corinthians 13:4-8

REFLECT

Jesus has loved you with a love that never ends.

RESPOND

Who is the person God is calling you to love like this? How can you tangibly express this love today?

PRAY

Lift to God that which is on your heart today.

Jesus said to Simon Peter, "Simon son of John, do you love me more than these?" He said to him, "Yes , Lord; you know that I love you." Jesus said to him, "Feed my lambs." A second time he said to him, "Simon son of John, do you love me?" He said to him, "Yes, Lord; you know that I love you." Jesus said to him, "Tend my sheep." He said to him the third time, "Simon son of John, do you love me?" Peter felt hurt because he said to him the third time, "Do you love me?" And he said to him, "Lord, you know everything; you know I love you." Jesus said to him, "Feed my sheep."
John 21:15-17

REFLECT

Jesus has loved us, fed us and given us all we need for life and ministry. He calls us to love and feed others in his name.

RESPOND

Who are the people God is calling you to feed as his sheep? Pray for them now and ask God to prepare them to receive his message.

PRAY

Lift to God that which is on your heart today.

Pray Daily: Igniting Our Passion for God

..."Lord, if another member of the church sins against me, how often should I forgive? As many as seven times?" Jesus said to him, "Not seven times, but I tell you, seventy-seven times."
Matthew 18:21-22

REFLECT

God offers us new mercies every day. How can I be more like God?

RESPOND

Whom do you need to forgive as God has forgiven you?

Lift to God that which is on your heart today.   PRAY

"EVERY GREAT MOVEMENT OF GOD CAN BE TRACED TO A KNEELING figure."
D.L. MOODY

Continue praying daily any passage from the Bible. Read the text. Repeat it. Then pose and answer questions such as:

How can I praise God for and through this?
What does this passage reveal about God and his Kingdom?
Lord, why have you brought these verses before me today?
If this truth were impressed upon my heart, how would I be changed?
What does this passage reveal about human nature? About me?
Holy Spirit, what wrong behavior, harmful emotions, or false attitudes come to me when I forget this truth?
How would my family, my friends, my church be different if we lived this truth?
What actions would we take if this truth were impressed upon our hearts?
Holy Spirit, does my life demonstrate that I am remembering and acting on this truth?

God is moving in and through you! Amen!